Thank you so much for all your efforts and support that you gave to me in past few months. I'm very happy to receive the book as it is my first time when my poem got published and I want thought to show my gratitude to you through this mail. Hope we get to work together again in the future and wishing you all the best for future endeavour 'ali Prasad

I am already a follower of page, since December 2020 a. enjoyable.- Swarnadip Chatte,

Hi there, I just wanted to say th ╷*er reading some of the poetry on Wingless Dreamer, I feel inspired and in awe. I've been writing on and off as a hobby for a few years now but seeing what you've done and how you've built this whole community of writers, I'm really inspired and impressed. You've given me just a bit more inspiration to keep working on my projects and for that I thank you.- Ryan*

Best of afternoons! I am Arnaldo Batista, author of the poem "Hypochondriac Thriving," that your publication has chosen to enter in your "Fruits of our Quarantine" contest. I am simply sending this email to first thank you for this as I am truly humbled by your decision to accept this poem for publication. I wrote this poem after many nights of night terrors and panic attacks due to my looming anxiety over the pandemic and instant changes the world is going through seemingly overnight. Your validation of this poem is received by such validation and a feeling of triumph that I cannot put into words, so genuinely, thank you. -Arnaldo Batista

Proud and grateful to be included in one of your previous books. I will purchase and help promote your continued good work- J Brooke

It took me so long to get into reading & writing poetry, but last summer, I finally felt inspired to do it. In December 2019, I was published for the first time as a poet!! My poem is featured in the winter edition of Passionate Penholders by @winglessdreamer1 (available on Amazon) Poetry is always so relaxing to me and I hope that during this time of "unknowns," hopefully, we can all be inspired to relax a little and curl up with some good poetry! It's finally here!!! I am officially a published author check it out for yourself on Amazon! Thank you @winglessdreamer1 for believing in my work! – Landri Driskill

Keep up this excellent work. Poetry truly connects the readers with poetic souls across countries and cultures – Amita Sanghvi

It is a great joy for me that a kindhearted editor of a journal like you has liked my poem. Thank you again. I am hundred percent willing to publish my poem, "Oh beautiful beloved" in The book issue called Diversity: There's a beauty in that too. I am pasting my updated bio below. Be happy in life this is my heartfelt wishes to you.-Sandip Saha

I truly admire their creative publication who works so hard to promote emerging writers and artists for what they truly deserve and make them feel much appreciated. Hats off.- Josh Sullivan

Unlike traditional publisher Wingless Dreamer has supported and encouraged me to a great extent. -Sowmyata Singh

Wingless Dreamer

CULTURAL REGENERATION THROUGH OUR
CREATIVE COMMUNITY

A GLASS OF WINE WITH EDGAR

Edited by

RUCHI ACHARYA

Book cover by

GIADA MANCINI

ABOUT US

The Wingless Dreamer Community was founded by Ruchi Acharya to bridge the gap between emerging writers or artists and traditional publishing. Ruchi's community is a global platform for those who truly believe in themselves and are passionate about writing or illustrating. It's the dream of her community to create a space where the authors or artists are free to express themselves.

Wingless Dreamer slowly but steadily grew with artists and writers from all over the world. Over time Wingless Dreamer became the main stage for well-known professional writers and artists to express themselves, all at the same place.

We envisioned a community where writers and artists would be invited to publish solely based on the merit of their writing and creative skills. The Wingless Dreamer community connects all essences of writing, illustrating, editing, marketing, and promoting on a single platform so that authors and illustrators don't have to go through the hardships of the publishing processes and focus on their work. The Community members become part of the family and are guided, supported, and encouraged on every step they make towards their writing and art career. The members can get access to free critiques, reviews, marketing, and in some cases funding for their work via email.

Our Wingless Dreamer team spends lots of time and energy to create as many contests as possible on different themes every quarter so that writers and artists can truly enjoy their experience with us.
The community is still growing and its accomplished authors and artists speak for themselves.

"Being a writer can sometimes be solitary and quiet. A writer can understand how it feels to fall in love with every single character, to battle with dialogues, to work with vivid poetic devices, to endeavor for perfection and to build an entire universe from scratch. Guess what? You're not alone. We understand the efforts you put every day into your work. Since we are a team of writers and artists too.

The art and writing industry is always considered as something obscure and profound by the public in general. It has become so difficult to stand alone and be noticed in the art industry or to stick with a writing career in the commercial society we live in today. Compared to other financial and economic-related jobs, things related to art are the minority.

Art and poetry are the most important elements of our life as it helps us understand and appreciate the world around us. No matter what anybody tells you words and ideas have the power to change the world and sneaks the truth upon you.

One of my favorite quotes:

We don't read and write poetry because it's cute. We read and write poetry because we are members of the human race. And the human race is filled with passion. And medicine, law, business, engineering, these are noble pursuits and necessary to sustain life. But poetry, beauty, romance, love, these are what we stay alive for.-N.H. Kleinbaum, Dead Poets Society

In the end I would like to urge all the people who are reading this to never ever give up on your dreams. Seize the day. Every day counts. You're art. Never step back from showing your creative side to the world. It's beautiful."

-Ruchi Acharya, Wingless Dreamer Founder

R. Acharya

-Ruchi Acharya

CONTENTS

For my family: my parents, Ramesh and Indra; my sister Samiksha; who all love nothing more than a good poetry collection, well told.

-Editor, Ruchi Acharya

Deep into that darkness peering, long I stood there, wondering, fearing, doubting, dreaming dreams no mortal ever dared to dream before.

-Edgar Allan Poe

1. THE CASTLE LIVES IN ME
(inspired by The conqueror worm, Spirits of the dead)

Shuffling and mumbling and finally disembarking
Granted passage by a long-dead man with a cane-branch
Creaking ferry condescending but never speaking
For the others those fellow travelers I'll avoid knowing
I wonder whether it would've been possible for me
Or for anyone to remain in that dubious place

With the torture chamber of blood-blackened wood and iron
The winding colony of faithless plots in secret passages
The curse of the Squire's daughter's lover
The crumpled butler deranged by loyalty into sadism
Oh and that locked chamber illuminated in crisp flame
Candelabras atop a most questionable and menacing altar

Now safe and exiled time has compressed behind me
And I'm no longer sidling down carpeted halls
Around cataphracts and peering portrait eyes
Such is my surprise to sometimes yearn
For the velvet melodies of those hoary floor clocks
And an angry sea quaking the bedrock with maledictions

TAYLOR SIPOS

Tay Sipos is a recent graduate who writes poetry, personal essays, and short stories. She has published in GCU Today magazine and within the Startlebloom Literary Review. These works include, "In Memoriam," "How I See Home," and "Rejoice." She is currently preparing a portfolio to apply for future creative writing master's programs.

2. YOU'RE MY LITTLE SHADOW
(inspired by Alone)

You're my little shadow,
always hovering around the edges of my mind.
    Sometimes I'm hovering around the edges of yours.

I want to take you with me everywhere,
pack you up and put you in my pocket.
    I am so in love with you.

You're my little shadow,
and I wish you could see me, but you're not looking.
    Sometimes I wonder if you even think about me.

I'm waiting for you to turn back and smile,
run toward me with your arms wide open.
    But I don't know if today's the right day for that.

You're my little shadow,
and I can't believe you don't see me here.
    Sometimes I can't even remember if we've really met.

I've been standing by your window for hours,
and it's really starting to get cold out here.
    Please let me be your little shadow.

LIZ DEGREGORIO

Liz DeGregorio is a writer and editor living in New York City. Her poems have been published in Indie Blu(e) Publishing's anthology "SMITTEN," Crack the Spine's anthology "Neighbors," Beyond Words Literary Magazine, Gravitas, Riva Collective's Chunk Lit and In Parentheses. Her flash fiction has appeared in *82 Review and Ruminate Magazine, and she's had fiction published in BUST Magazine.

3. LOVE IS THE WEAPON
(inspired by The Raven)

Love is the weapon. It's the knife I turn
In an open wound; it's the rope I tighten
Round a man's warm neck; it's the shotgun
I load with a twelve bore shell. Are you frightened?
You should be. I mark men forever with traces
Of possession that never fade—they can
Think only of me and of my many faces
For whatever remains of their lives: an
Obsession that never relaxes
And can never max out. Hear that roar?
It's the sound of thousands collapsing
In despair because the woman they adore

Remains beyond their touch, yet stands before
Their eyes to release them nevermore.

DUNCAN WU

Duncan Wu is Raymond A Wagner Professor of Literary Studies at Georgetown University, Washington, DC. He is a former fellow of St Catherine's College, Oxford and is best known for his anthology of British Romantic texts, Romanticism. His anthology of poetry about dogs, Dog Eared, will be published by Basic Books in October 2020.

4. BIRD
(inspired by The Raven)

Bird! that sings me out of bedrock
    from my dreams of blissful wedlock
Dreams of sweets and treats assuring
    days replete with golden mooring
Worlds where Love's sweet breath caresses
    hats and boots and silken dresses
Sleep, so sacred thus restoring
    heartache's balm when grief is pouring
Bird! Why did you break my snoring? Bird! This heart of mine imploring!
But soft, your song! My soul is soaring!

Bird! Why aren't you singing bright now?
    Still and dull, the day's a blight now
Thought seems fraught and mind is fickle
    fat and dull, and taste, a pickle!
Drapes of lead and floors smell cheesy,
    rooms so vast, hearts ill and queasy
All around Death's cloak and sickle,
    creek and stream turn but to trickle
Bird! Break through this bleak drab nickel! Sing all day and night with mickle!
But soft, you stir! My soul's a-tickle!

ELIZABETH LOGUN

Elizabeth Logun is a playwright, short story writer and poet. Her plays have been produced in New York and Los Angeles, and she is the recent 3rd place winner of the Inaugural James Stevenson Award for one of her short plays. She also writes for animation. She is a contributing writer/performer to EST/LA's True Story and is a published poet. She has also served as a theatre teaching artist for under-served youth in Los Angeles.

5. RITUAL
(inspired by Fairy-land and The Haunted Palace)

Speak the words with gusto
Oxidized metal,
infernal threshold

Rinse thy hands

As if they're not already sullied
covetous pen strokes
dripping with honey

ceramic viscera brimming
with malignant intent
Trim the worms silk
raise earth up from the cement
Now gather your ilk
and speak the words to be said.

We pay the price to know
Seated full lotus high above note
Head of ram
Crown encircles skull of goat
Dripping stalactites thoughts clad in chrome
Light the candles
Then pay the price to know

As above,
So is below.

ALEXANDER GRUTZA

Alexander is a Bartender and aspiring Poet from Brooklyn, New York who hopes to expand his creative horizons and continue his journey in writing in whatever form it takes.

6. GOOD NIGHT, AND GOOD LUCK
(inspired by The Tell-Tale Heart)

It's been seven days and I feel so weak
I been walk-talkin, doin all this in my sleep
still I keep pushin myself to see how high I reach
see how much more before disease release,
just trying to keep up with my shadow
somehow there's a road less traveled than
the one not yet built—include the notes on
how to exclude myself and load
some cunning interpretation of
the best way to say this—maybe I
can't say this? Maybe I've created
a mistaken worst-case elaboration
on my expectations, maybe I've lost
myself in the translatin frustratin akin
to something like how I've tried my best to
repent for these sins—how I've lied to
make sense of some things, how I've
climbed my way out from beneath the
foundation and sent my message in
poetic interpolation—sign off, station.

ANTHONY MIRARCKI

Anthony Mirarcki lives in Syracuse, New York, with his wife. He currently works as a carpenter and is a full-time student at Oswego State University, working towards his BA in English and Creative Writing. Anthony's work has appeared in LIT Magazine, the Great Lake Review, the 2020 anthology Poems from the Lockdown, and has earned honorable mention in the 47th New Millennium Writing Awards.

7. RUNNING WITH THE DEAD
(inspired by Dream-land)

I run
through
the cemeteries

the tombstones
& mausoleums

speak nothing
say everything

you need to know
about a dead man

white lilies
standing upright

the breeze
light

but there
is no sound

the tombstones
& mausoleums

speak nothing
say everything

you need to know
about a dead man

CHAD W. LUTZ

Chad W. Lutz is a speedy, non-binary writer born in Akron, Ohio, in 1986 and raised in the neighboring suburb of Stow. They graduated from Kent State University with their BA in English in 2008 and from Mills College in Oakland, California, with their MFA in Creative Writing in 2018. Their first book, For the Time Being, is currently available through J. New Books.

8. WHEN YOU ARE THE LIBRARIAN OF DIFFIDENCE
(inspired by The Haunted Palace)

You live your days asphyxiating-
Nothing is worse than to be
a slave with a tongue that has been cut
out of insecurity that makes one's flesh crawl
off the bone- showing we are all the same.

Your striving to be recognize-
Able Ego isn't quick-
lime for scurvy from self-
inflicted wounds from your hand
the one you were dealt

Is it better now-
you see no individual-
identity stolen by Death's mag-
got who will catalogue your anonymity
that you feared in life.

Do you really still want to be on the shelf-
life is not worth saving when you are a
lone being who has realized that.
We are all just sitting in the stacks
waiting to be read by a god we do not know

ANTHONY CHESTERFIELD

Anthony Chesterfield is a social worker who specializes in end-of-life care and hospice. Each of his patients and their families have individually taught him about the unknown as he continues his vocation. His published works include, Death's Strife, available at Amazon.com and Barnes & Noble. Anthony's poem N-95 was also published in Poems from the Lockdown by Willowdown Books, and his poem, Nursing Home Under Siege, is published in Poet's Choice. His poem Essential Alcohol was recently published in Whispers to Roars. Anthony considers fatherhood to be the greatest adventure of his life, and believes there is no one perfect way to be a father. He is currently pursuing an MFA at Manhattanville College, and lives in NY, with his wife, three daughters, and three cats.

9. RANCID
(inspired by The Tell-Tale Heart)

cast-iron brambles kindle in rage
our hearts left broken in moans
solace arcs amid dim screams
my love, sweet Lily, so dear

faint howls beneath a feather pillow
arouses and inflames a throttling heat
your fragrance hovers so foul
my Lily, oh Lily, my dear

quarried lodge in a murky abyss
my conundrum embraced and fleeced
raven in tune with sweet baby's cries
sleep Lily, dead Lily, my dear

STEVEN WIGHT

Steven Wight is from Walnut Creek, California. He has written two novels along with numerous short stories, memoirs, and the occasional poem. In 2019, he earned first place in The League of Utah Writer's First Chapter contest for his novel, Annie on the Run. In 2017 he completed his Post Baccalaureate certificate in writing from U. C. Berkeley. His short story, The Haunted Castle,' was recently published by Wingless Dreamer in their book of poetry, 'My Father and I.'

10. HOODOO
(inspired by The Cask of Amantillado, The Black Cat and The Tell-Tale Heart)

"Mercy! Such old hoodoo! Hopelessly second-rate.
At some drawing's or painting's edge, a slab bearing the artist's name
or initials, the dates of his birth and death. Delightful!

"Or that museum piece: his back to us, its brooding great
genius stands on a mountaintop till later each night
when no one sees: presto! Voila! The crag's now bare.

"Or consider your portrait's eerily happy likeness
but as we came downstairs this morning appeared slightly
changed. The lips? And yes! its eyes: someone's been scared."

Beneath his final work, the infrared located
its first model, who must have pleased his eye—in quite
a different pose, strapped into a restraint chair,

both which he covered with a wall that also hides
the light and a small barred window through which it glared—
shining from the camp's tower behind her frantic gaze.

MARK MANSFIELD

Mark Mansfield is the author of two full-length collections of poetry, Strangers Like You (2008, revised 2018, Chester River Press) and Soul Barker (2017, Chester River Press). His poems have appeared in The Adirondack Review, Bayou, Fourteen Hills, Iota, The Journal, Magma Poetry, Measure, Salt Hill Journal, Star*Line, and elsewhere. He was a recent Pushcart Prize nominee. Currently, he lives in upstate New York.

11. WHY WE MUST HURT THE ONES WE LOVE
(inspired by *The Conqueror Worm*)

My eyes are reservoirs of lead,
gray, molten, thin enough to slosh
when a check is late, or the rent's due,
or something's lost, or something's horribly found.
I wake, holding the razor to my neck
when you don't say the words
exactly as I must hear them.
I've seen you turn, exhausted, clipped
right where I want you, when you think
I might do it. My mind's all wrong.
It's happening it's happening.
I pad from room to room.
We're here, it and I. Watch: I will make of it
an autonomous thing, a way
to avoid the blame, a pitiful defining
of Marcos and his demon and their dance.

MARCOS VILLATORO

Marcos Villatoro is the author of several novels, two collections of poetry and a memoir. His Romilia Chacón crime fiction series has been translated into Japanese, German, Portuguese and Russian. He has written and performed essays on PBS and NPR. His latest work has appeared in the Los Angeles Times, the Wall Street Journal and the New York Times. After living several years in Central America, Marcos moved to Los Angeles, where he teaches literature at Mount. St. Mary's University.

12. PLAGUE TEN
(inspired by The City in the Sea)

Even the dry cleaners smiling
at the proffered ticket,
the coffee order up, even
dog leashes splayed like hands,
the endless human cram, echoes
the glad news of your death.

JOSHUA THUSAT

Joshua Thusat was born in Port Clinton, Ohio. He received his graduate degree in English from Bowling Green State University. Currently, he teaches English in the Chicagoland area.

13. I WILL NOT DIE BEFORE I WAKE
(inspired by A Dream)

I toss and turn in my bed. I hit a wall. It is made of wood. Above me is more wood. I feel like I am in a box. I push everywhere and scream. *I am not in my bed.* Hear voices from above. *I am underground.* I scream for help. No one hears my screams. *No one hears my cries.* Why am I here? What has happened to me? How did I get here? Why can't anyone hear me? *Am I dead?* I'm not meant to be here. I'm needed. Someone needs me. I don't want to hear anymore crying. *I must get out.* Close my eyes. *Pray to God to set me free.* Close my fist. Punch the wood above me. Knuckles turned red. Knuckles bleed. Punch to an open hole. Knuckles sore and bloody. Like winning a boxing match to make the final knockout. Dirt falls. Crawl through the dirt. Climb up to the top. *I was in my room. Finally, home.*

STACY VARGAS

Stacy Vargas was born and raised in Brooklyn, NY. She is currently a student in the MFA program at St. Francis College where she will graduate this summer. In May 2018, she self-published a collection of poems: Fight, Survive, Thrive.

14. SCAPEGOAT
(inspired by The City in the Sea and Lenore)

Unworthy was a tattoo
carved into her chest
by an orange, rusty nail.

In a tiny coastal town
boastful of their large lilacs and ornate steeples
she was forced to forage for morsels
from men's plates,
Made with imitation love.

She was given enough to live,
but not enough to leave;
The town required a reminder
That well-being came at a cost.

J.J. COLE

J. J. is a poet who lives in the beautiful seacoast of New Hampshire with his lovely wife and
two amazing daughters. They enjoy the New England outdoors in all seasons. When he's not
writing he enjoys the smell of a good book, the challenge of a thoughtful puzzle, and the
taste of food cooked without recipes. His poems have previously appeared in Typishly, Basil
O'Flaherty, Rat's Ass Review, and Prachya Review.

15. EXPANSIVE LOVE
(inspired by Alone)

My love for you is impeccable.
It stands on bloody stumps.
Splatters razored sentiments
with a tongue ripped out by its root.
A victim of your infernal inertia,
I danced fandangos
as you iced me unblinking.
Expecting more and better,
I drown in your cesspool,
cavorting to get your attention.
Your hushed agony,
locked in holy secret
in the imagined center,
secure in sphere upon sphere
of protective custody.
And I,
wanting only a droplet
of you on my parched lips
to satisfy a thirst
for expansive love.

BRUCE EDELMAN

"I am a retired teacher of writing and English. Writing poetry and fiction take up all of my time".-Bruce

16. NOBLE STRANGER
(inspired by Annabel Lee)

Silently I stood there watching and waiting on this earthly plane
Without emotion or empathy I wandered this place
A place of torment, a place of madness, a place of disdain
Peering through the shadows I observed a world on fire
Endless mortals blind to the carnage and consumed by games
In awe as I smiled through the pyros and danced in the flames

Envious eyes, hateful spirits of man
So eager to kick a poor gent into the sand
Love is temporary, love isn't kind
To run amok blindly just to be killed every time
Fools I say, fools I declare
Love has no rewind
Hope is unfair

Run to the shore
The shore by the sea
Evade the countless hearts
The sirens singing to deceive thee
Continue along the coast and never succumb to their beauty
Unless noble stranger
You become me

ANANIAS REESE

Ananias Reese is an aspiring poet and musician from Augusta, Georgia. He studied Criminal Justice and Psychology at Georgia Military College. He finds purpose in writing poetry, and music. He believes there is hope, beauty, pain as well as horrors in this world and he spends his life writing about it whenever he can.

17. STEPBROTHER
(inspired by Dream-land)

I often dream of my father's house,
and the only pine out front
not cut down—the stumps of the others,
markers of rot. I'm always standing atop
the moon's filtered, scattering of light
when I hear the garage opening. Someone
knows I'm quitting. The tree's needled
branches are hung with shadows, maybe
ones that I know, begging the sky,
as I am, for flight. The sky says nothing
but clouds too thin to hide the moon;
so I reach for the closest branch, and pull.
Each new height leaves me sticky until
the tree deflates, my jumping off point
becoming as small as me, and I swear
if I could get higher than these houses,
then I would float past and into a mossy farness,
out to my mother, homeless, somewhere.
The trunk is so short now
that I balance on its tip just one step
from the ground, and of course I fall,
but the falling is not just one step.
Each branch pushes above me,
away from me until I land at stepbrother's feet.
Knees bend slowly above me,
hands are on my breasts, my head
jammed into the pine's roots.
He doesn't say sorry until I'm bleeding,
until my eyes meet the moon and reflect.

CLOE WATSON

Cloe Watson is a second year student in Bowling Green State University's MFA program. Her work has appeared in Defunkt Magazine, Beyond Words Literary Magazine and Ohio's Best Emerging Poets.

18. POEM FOR A MURDER
(inspired by Alone)

The neighbors are sleeping just down the hall
Trapped in illusions a thousand feet tall
But I am here now, with this knife in my chest
A thrum in my head, and a prayer in my breast
As he jerks it out and thrusts it back in
I wonder where death is and how it begins
Does it start with a bang, a rattle, a clang?
Or is it a lullaby a young mother sang?
Perhaps it is silence, a long sullen void
Or maybe it's violent, a sculpture destroyed
Whatever it is, whatever it may be
It's coming here soon, so soon I will see
I've seen it before, such red on this bed
And I'll see it again, when this day turns dead
I never imagined an end quite like this
So far from the people I know that I'll miss
I never imagined an end quite like this
My body a minefield and holey like swiss
I never imagined an end quite like this
Lukewarm and soggy and deader than piss
But an end is an end, and an end it shall be
I did not seek out this end, no, it came to meet me

AMBER GRACI

Amber Graci is a twenty-eight year old poet from Charlotte, North Carolina, currently residing in Alcova, Illinois, where she works as an editor for Kettlebrook Press.

19. AMBER CLAD HEART
(inspired by Alone)

Autumn's march and the trees bled, crying a tear slow to fall.

Leaves tarnish in the ache of summer's steady exodus.

The birds nestle in while the wind is sharp on the skin,
like a razor through your jacket.

And through the passage of the slowing wood,
the pine kept the green upon this forest true.

The crunch beneath the foot and the dance,
deadened leaves in the stale wind.

And for ten thousand years my heart sunk in the sap,
beneath a loving pine.
Curing in the pool,
from the dripping tears I held in my mind.
Culminating on my heart solidifying the node.

To the hard amber stone plopped quietly in a chest,
beating behind the rock-
the rhythm of distress.

SKYLER WALKER

Skyler is an active poet but a full time Electrician. Native American of the Ho-Chunk tribe in Nebraska who is a hopeful upcoming voice in poetry. He's a yet-to-be published poet and his favorite poem of Poe's would be "Alone".

20. BURIAL
(inspired by The Haunted Palace)

Once upon a time we were space dust
falling from stars.
Now we are rotted and put in the ground
Never to return to our celestial home
Our souls left to dream of the brains
we once possessed.
Even the chemicals of preservation
are no match for parasitic bacteria,
which consumes our stardust.
Who are you?
But a corpse once warm
Did you forget your place?
As have I
We wither
We die
Our corpses remain shy
Until dust in silk lined boxes
that refuse to release us,
back to our natural state.
Of dusty stars grounded
by this gravity.

HEATHER RUSSELL

HD Russell is a poet and author with one book of fiction and poetry in publication. She also had a poem published in her college literary magazine Echoes and Images. She lives and writes in the southern United States.

21. THE BLEAK HARVEST

When the clouds fell from the sky,
and the last birds sang their tune,
The swilling seas churned dark with bile, and nothing was in bloom.

When the final church bells tolled, people cried to pray.
But bleakness hung upon the line there was nothing left to say.

Silence fell across all things, but far beyond the pale,
I saw our mother all in black behind the darkened veil.

She cried out for her children, who'd left her for the road.
She thought we'd offer alms for her, but for the seeds we sowed.

When all was dark across the land, and we all longed for home,
resounding calls were sent for her, but all's left was just her tome.

MARY GANGENES

Mary Gangenes is a poet and author based in Santa Barbara, CA. She has a has worked in arts marketing for the past 20 years. She received her Bachelor of Arts (B.A.) focused in English Language and Literature, from UC Santa Barbara.

22. A SONNET FOR THE UNKNOWN
(inspired by The Raven and Alone)

A love song sweet as berries on the vine
Graces my ears, but yet escapes my eyes.
What bird, what feathered devil's song does whine
To haunt the dawn with splendid, wooing cries?
Whose mouth is crafting melodies that shriek
Eternal in my mind and memory
'Til nothing but the clacking of its beak
Exists within my tortured reverie?
The name, the name, naught matters but the name!
What cuckoo, robin, chickadee, or jay,
Greenfinch, swallow, lark, or warbler is to blame
My pining ev'ry precious day away?
But sing again, yes sing 'til I'm insane!
Rejoice, or all my grief will be in vain!

MADALYN DALY

I am an Asian-American writer and actor from the Seattle area. I don't have any fun writing credits to cite for myself, but this one time my fourth grade teacher was really impressed with my poem about beets. Since then, I have been writing poetry primarily exploring uncertainty. Much of my work draws from surrealism and dada, and seeks to recreate and explore the feelings of discomfort in our personal identities that I believe is universal. - Madalyn

23. THE MALL AT 10 A.M.
(inspired by The Haunted Palace)

Smudged glass displays a party
no one was invited to.

Inside, jackets hang
like bats (red, green, blue, purple, gray, blue)

waiting. Among a sea
of other things

mannequins cock shoulders
as if to tell you

how lovely it is
wearing big jewelry,

bearing your stomach,
feeling no shame.

Perfumes mix, thick, a soup
in the air—chemical sweet.

Models smile wildly,
cardboard-trapped,

each shining paper eye
following me

as I go empty-handed,
and music thumps softly for no one.

CASSANDRA BALIGA

Cassandra Baliga is a graduate of Purdue University Fort Wayne with a B.A. in English. She's had work previously appear in The Red Booth Review, Confluence, and ANGLES and is a two-time winner of the DeKalb Snowbound Writer's Poetry Contest.

24. SILENT SOLSTICE
(inspired by The Raven)

Once upon a yuletide dreary, while I pondered tired and teary,
Stacks and piles of half-wrapped Christmas gifts about me on the floor,
While I sat there, nearly crying, suddenly I heard the prying
Sound of someone softly trying to unlock the kitchen door.
"Only Gregory," I snuffled, feeling lower than before,
"Only Greg, and nothing more."

Greg marched in and saw the gold chains, drums, computer, dresses,
toy trains, Gifts for all his fam'ly spread around me on the oak-hard
floor--
"What?" he yelled. "Not finished, Trudy? Mother sent hers out last
Tuesday! Sis needs hers by Monday morning" (they're escaping to the
shore).
"Brother Mike's away on Sunday" (to Korea with the Corps).
"Bud wants his the day before."

He continued, tone demanding, "What's for dinner? Here I'm standing,
Waiting while you fiddle with a job that's simple for a moron--"
At which point I stuck him with the scissors that I'd (oh, so deftly)
Used to wrap the gifts for Michael, Mother Ann, and Bud and
Lauren. . . . Blessed silence reigned as I crammed Greg into a box that
bore an
Icon of an apple core.

SUSAN CUMMINS MILLER

Tucson author SUSAN CUMMINS MILLER is a recovering field geologist and college instructor. She compiled and edited A SWEET, SEPARATE INTIMACY: WOMEN WRITERS OF THE AMERICAN FRONTIER, 1800-1922, and writes the Frankie MacFarlane, Geologist, mysteries. Miller's poems have appeared in numerous journals and anthologies, including 2020's What We Talk About When We Talk About It: Variations on the Theme of Love, v. I, II, and the forthcoming Unstrung and The Write Launch.

25. PREPOST PAN
(inspired by Alone)

Hello, old friend, which I have not seen nor spoken to in half a year. Half a year feeling like half a lifetime inside a lifetime inside of a fallen star. I once saw you daily, every moment, every second, we blinked together, breathed in unison, and collaborated about the what-ifs and why- nots and floated through our days with a simple arrogance of unimportance that now feels like a slow drip of melancholy increasingly slowed by an impending chill. Now we are apart, divided by miles of unseen maladies, foes, fears. Driven father away from the sweet succulence of nothing in particular, a dance in the wind, a carefree and careless twirl with a stranger. A coffee in a crowd, a flash of a smile in a plaza, a night time whispering in a field of dreamers. No more do we dance in unison, twirling toward the monotonous beauty of a Monday, the regret of a Sunday, the fire of a new day. No longer do we book and plan and run and share and sip and stare, into a horizon of endless hopes and nearly not one scare. I can see you in the mirror, a glimpse of a ghost in a shadow that once was. I spy you for a brief second and my heart flutters, gasps, hopes... but you disappear into the shadow and I know you were never there. My closed eyes can see you, hear you, smell you, taste you, but upon opening the vision fades as quickly as it came, leaving me gasping, breathless, hopeless, helpless. With sadness you slip farther and farther away, as each day brings new meters of angry oceans between us, swirling with sharp scraping teeth that grow on creatures multiplying within its depths. No boat will reunite us, no ship can pull us back to the shores of before. The lighthouse that guided our collective travels has toppled, its blazing beacon frayed and fizzled, crashed into the vicious waves that fought to pull it down, a soundless splash as it sank into its watery grave. I do not have the courage to find you again, to battle the turbulent sea and its tangles of weeds and its gnashing beasts that cut away my courage. I will not try, as to find you would be too painful a reminder of a calmer sea, filled with sparkling hope and a beautiful void. I dream of seeing you again, under the same sun that touched our crowns when we did not live a thousand lives in a hundred horrible days. I would hold you tight, our energies merging, swirling upward, a great arm of new strength and hope pulling us upward, above the air and into the heavens above all the peril and perished promises of people. We would stare into each other's eyes, seeing aging beyond years and wisdom beyond measure but a new element that is hope that can only grow out of a great and mighty despair. And at that moment we would know we were never apart, we were always there, just blinded by fear and distraction. We have always been one, you and I. You are the childlike me, the *me* who ran across mountains with lungs full of air. You did not leave me, you were hiding, waiting, for this monster under the bed to fade into the morning light. You were keeping yourself safe. We were always together, but you were never safe. We were never safe.

LISA STEWART

Lisa is an emerging writer enrolled in her MFA. She spends her time pondering life while balancing a medley of pets, adult children and the evolving facets of everyday life in a pandemic in New York.

26. A STILLBIRTH
(inspired by Alone)

I feel that I'll live forever
but in a cold way and in tangents

as the blue frame of a poem
or a stain on a cotton sheet

eaten by moths

we have all seen something wrong

a rabbit's foot pressed down into the road
or a foaming mouth
or teeth coated all over in skin

(all who witness death must die)

we cannot prove a lifespan
any more than we can prove a God

I've coughed up blood but
does that mean I have veins

or that I am fluid inside—
a pool held by tarp

from the winter outside
am I skin and tendons stretching

or an aging image of somebody else

CAITLIN DUNN

I have a BFA in Creative Writing from Belhaven University. Several of my poems have been published in Belhaven's literary magazine The Brogue and in the High Shelf Literary Journal. My poems have won the Live Poets' Society of New Jersey poetry contest and the Southern Literary Award.-Caitlin

27. CROOKED SMILE
(inspired by Evening Star)

Dark thistle spurts from the earth,
your long feet crush the ripe plum barbs.
Silvery tangs of anger stenches
the air around us. You cut me
with your gaze. Your hands paint
blue—purple—yellow hues
under my swelling lips, above my strained brow.
I am your canvas. Your masterpiece.

You rip each molar from your slanted mouth.
Hands shaking, nails scraping against layers of bloody
gum. Simply because I loved that crooked smile of yours.

I crawl along the mud, grit seeping through the skins of my knees.
I collect each jagged tooth, the broken bones slicing my palms red.
I dig, nails tearing along the rocks and dirt.
Pheretima earthworms squirm against my skin.
Roots stretch along my blood-filled veins,
clawing forever towards the dark damp of the earth.
Folding over my knees, like a graying leaf, I lay each tooth around
me—
a broken smile.

I still love that crooked smile.

MASHAELA FARRIS

Mashaela Farris is a graduate student at Weber State University. Her prose and poems have been published in Utah Valley University's undergraduate journals, Warp & Weave and Touchstones. She enjoys hiking with her hound dog and noting the intricate details of nature.

28. FOREVER AFTER
(inspired by Spirits of the Dead)

Do you see them? She points,
beyond my shoulder, behind,
above. *There. And there. Do*
you see them?

Beyond her cold, metal bedrails
I imagine Onyx shot with orange and
green. Silver fulminate and copper.
Poof! *Do you*
see them?

Chairs, she says, pointing.
Over there. Floating.
Hospital curtain, bland
tan span. This room. And
the next. All the same.
Do you see them?

I shake my head. No chairs,
nothing floating, except fluttering
lost bird of my heart. Bland
tan span then bedpan,
lifespan. *Do you see?*

Caravan of chairs, floating,
the procession of cars, headlights,
soft grass, clumped thump
of shovels, prayers.
Floating, beyond.
Do you see
them?

TERRY COX-JOSEPH

Terry Cox-Joseph is a former newspaper reporter and editor. From 1994-2004 she was the coordinator for the Christopher Newport University Writers' Conference. Her first chapbook, "Between Then and Now," was published by Finishing Line Press in 2018. She is the president of the Poetry Society of Virginia.

29. BAUDELAIRE

(inspired by French poet Charles Baudelaire who translated Poe's work)

Baudelaire, you beautiful man,
You gorgeous soul!
You were a Shakespeare and Mozart
Combined with a vampire.
You were a proud ship sailing toward the horizon,
And a descending aircraft ripping toward Hell.
Your eyes were ever intoxicated with divine light,
Your heart intractably drunk with sin's wine.
In white clouds of opiate smoke you dreamt.
You were condemned to see sunsets in all,
Damned by the stars, and women.
Samson would concur, as Villon,
And van Gogh.
Man of roses, yet satanic.
You were life, and death.
You were pink, blue, black.
Your mind was a cemetery
In which you strolled
Among flowers and skulls.
You turned French poetry
Into somber, Catholic
Music for evenings.
You are the King of poets,
Next to your son, Rimbaud.

B.R. BURDETTE

I am a poet from CA, US. My poems have been published in several literary journals, including the 15th Annual of Oberon Poetry. My upcoming publications will be in Lancelot Schaubert's Showbear Family Circus and Issue 16 of La Piccioletta Barca. B. R. Burdette

30. THE LONG DEFEAT
(inspired by Spirits of the Dead)

Welcome son, to the long defeat,
The battle at the edge of time.
What do you see out in the bleak?
Things left unrecorded in rhyme.

Arm yourself with guard-blade and shield,
And march onward into the fray.
When the fell things howl, don't you yield;
If you long to taste a new day.

Who is our foe, father tell me?
Who shall I face at march's end?
Is their armor thick, do they flee
Or do the stand and never bend.

Son, I cannot say, lest you break
But for now I'd savor your breath.
For the enemy comes with haste
And brings with him our last foe, DEATH.

RYAN DIAZ

Ryan Diaz is a writer, lecturer, and lay-theologian from Queens, NY. He holds a BA in History from St. Johns University and is completing a MA in Biblical Studies with Reformed Theological Seminary NYC. Ryan's work has been featured in the Scribble Literary Journal and The Washington Institute. He currently lives in Long Island, NY with his wife Janiece. Ryan is a fan of high fantasy, a coffee aficionado, and loves a good cigar.

31. BODIES OF WATER
(inspired by The River and A Descent Into the Maelstrom)

Walking the bright, windblown shore
cluttered with families, I purposely stray
into the hungry fingers of receding waves.

I abandon my shoes to clamber up the nearest rock face
to straddle a corner crag, sandy footed and
sun soaked, legs dangling, shading my eyes to gaze out to sea.

Intruding on my peripheral, I see her.
Ragged ribbons of hair, bare limbs, too thick for what must have been
her once slender frame, now an overstuffed rag doll.

Spread eagled and face down, shedding her fleshy casing,
she bumps playfully at the rocks just beneath my naked feet,
pin wheeling in the current.

I yank my legs up and away from her, cutting them
on the crag, imagining she might rise up
to catch my feet in her water fattened fingers.

Below me on the sand beachgoers are shouting.
A woman screams over and over and over.

The sky tilts left, then slides away,
white, red and shining.

N.M. BROWNLEE

N. M. Brownlee is an author, vocalist, travel addict and sci-fi enthusiast. She enjoys dance, nature, music and preparing her grandmother's recipe for jambalaya. She lives in California with her husband and one loud-mouth yet lovable cat.

32. ANTI-PSYCHIATRY
(inspired by The Raven)

I

You can say all you want about artistic men who
Cut off their ears but it is the sick society which
Invented psychiatry and diagnosed the collective spell cast On
Hölderlin and Monsieur de Nerval.

II

Edgar Allen Poe was not mad indeed at all
But is accused by these drasted psychiatrists
Of cerebral ill, these crowd of fools with not a fingertip Of genius
between them. It is rather downright dishonesty

III

To discredit the truth he sought to reveal. Did they not Even hit him on
his very head one night to make him forget That he was a genuine
lunatic? Thus, was a spell cast too On Monsieur Poe. But it couldn't
last.

IV

So, let us raise a suspicious hypothesis. That the poet
Is a seer that society cannot forebear. This is the puss that Must be
arraigned. As with Dr. Lacan whose diagnosis
Of poor old Artaud in Paris murdered his beautiful art with

V

Electroshock. Within the convulsed cell at Rodez where took place The
coma lasting fifteen minutes and the body wrung out
Twisted. If art dies there it must desperately fight back to
Breathe. It must grope for blind spots to REVOLT.

JONES IRWIN

I have taught philosophy in Dublin since 2001. I have published several monographs on philosophy and aesthetics and have published poetry most recently in Poetry London and Showbear Family Circus. My creative nonfiction was also recently published in Kairos magazine and my flash fiction was shortlisted for the Bridport Prize. This summer I have published a fiction in The Decadent Review and I am a featured poet in the next issue of Passengers Journal. I am also currently preparing a book on existential themes, to be published with Routledge in early 2021.-Jones

33. WHAT LIVES HERE?
(inspired by The Raven)

There is a rat that lives here, beneath my feet.
I hear its fine hair.
I can hear its scream.

Forgive my shouts! It wasn't me. Enter not and let me be.

I see the claws,
the marks on the floor.
I live in those lines,
the ones that mark the floor.

In and out,
it claims its hole. The one in the wall. The one in my soul.

See the rat,
how it moves.
It wants my words, the ones they want.

I know the cracks, the fractures in place. It split my head. The rat ate
my face.

My brain, my tongue
my eyes, my teeth.

Tell me,
Have you seen it? The rat that lives here, beneath my feet.
I can hear its fine hair.

I can hear it scream.

FRANCISCA RIBAR

Francisca has a deceptively boring writing process that includes her prized beats headphones and a box of cheddar goldfish. She is currently focused on writing her book but finds time to work on her collection of poems. She is a student and looks forward to the day she sees her work on bookshelves around the world.

34. ONE-NIGHTER
(inspired by A Dream within a Dream and The Sleeper)

Her parted lips –
entrance to a dank cave.
Her tongue –
a snake wriggling from her throat. Breasts
like African anthills.
And down lower –
a hairy portal to Hell.

In dead of night
I woke from demented dreams
to a desert windstorm
raging outside the motel window.

Alone.

TERRY CHESS

Previous work has appeared in The Chiron Review, Brickplight, Time Times 3, and Black Petals. When not writing, I collect rare books, read voraciously, and am an avid Chess player. I live in a suburb of Chicago, Illinois USA with my wife, and our Cavalier King Charles Spaniel, "Charlie".

35. LANDLORD'S LAMENT
(inspired by Alone)

My head is full of boxes.
Those boxes—full
of *smaller boxes yet*—
are apartments for these demons
I keep.

It's complex.

And though it's taken some time,
I think I'm finally onto their game.
I know they've been conspiring and
suspect that they wish to kill me—
individually or collectively.
Whatever it takes.

Even so
they're a lovely lot
these demon tenants of mine.
They speak so sweetly
and make such strong cases for themselves—
artful and impenetrable.

Just the other day I caught one on the 23rd floor
running down the hallway with scissors.
Dangerous? she purred.
No, no. That's just an old wives' tale.
Truth is, it's a lot of fun.

So I tried it.

Wound up plooking myself in the guts.
Took five stitches to make me whole again.

They'll do you that way.

But they're a steady bunch.
So dependable, so consistent.
They always pay the rent on time.
Even so, I know
someday soon I'll have to
kick them to the bricks.

All of them.

It's that or let them tear the place
apart—board by board—
smiling all the while.

CURT ALDERSON

CURT ALDERSON has been writing poetry and short stories for over 20 years. His work has appeared in print and online in Aura Literary Arts Review, Artemis, Spoken War, The Fertile Source, Red Crow, and elsewhere. He holds a Master's Degree in American Literature. He lives with his wife and two sons in a small, rural community outside of Roanoke, Virginia.

36. UNDER THE SURFACE
(inspired by The Conqueror Worm)

I don't recall
The slide into this mind
This exchange of brains

Who stole my thoughts
Replaced them with worms
Wiggles of worry that
Seek solace in dirt

Oh, how I wish a fish
Would swallow me whole

CATHLENE N. BUCHHOLZ

Cathlene N. Buchholz is a freelance writer and former anesthesia technician. Her writing has been featured in Cooked to Death: Volume II, Festival of Crime, Tonka Times magazine, Murmurs of the Past: An Anthology of Poetry and Prose, and a forthcoming mystery anthology titled Minnesota Not So Nice: Eighteen Tales of Bad Behavior. Cathlene lives on a hobby farm in Central Minnesota with her husband, one vision and hearing-challenged dog, and five sophisticated felines.

37. IF WALLS HAD TEARS

If these walls could talk
They would speak over each other
You wouldn't get a word in
There's too much to say

But when these walls housed them
They didn't dare speak
It was all left unsaid
But that was their way

Scars held hands down to the floor
They didn't dare move
They just stayed still
And the walls showed their years

The walls want to scream
And crash down on the dark
But they know they won't
What if no one even hears

The walls said silent prayers
That they would disappear
But for now they didn't speak
The walls voice was their tears

M.L.J. PLUTO

MLJ Pluto is a freelance writer who began her career in journalism. She took the promised "cheaper and easier" route and totally went off the intended path. She is enjoying finding the way back and also taking long walks, reading (of course) and traveling (hopefully again soon).

38. WHITE BEAR WOMAN
(inspired by A Dream within a Dream)

White Bear Woman Ode to Pfc Lori Ann Piestewa: First Native
American woman to die in combat during the Iraq War.

Metal scrapes sandy landscapes whirring.
Her heart falls there and breaks into crystalline slivers, candy.
Yes, like candy, because girls are made of sugar and spice.
Hearts don't pick up grenades and pull the pins.
She places a piece in her mouth and tastes the graininess,
rolls it in circles between her teeth and tongue and
it becomes tart, then sour, then gone.
Click. Click. Click
The rifle grip on her M16 is too slippery with sweat
she fumbles, chapped hands twisting and wringing up the stock.
Her finger falls there, lightly, lightly, on the trigger, lightly, lightly.
 Click. Click. Click.
Bullet jammed in the chamber, slaps magazine, fingers pulling,
pulling hard on the charging handle, they spring up, out of the chamber,
heated metal jewels burning marks like hickies on her forearms, she
lets go
charging handle settling back into place, dust cover closed, safety off,
semi.
Click. Click. Click.
Still jammed, one hand on the M16, the other on the wheel of the
Humvee. Sun streams through small glass cracked holes and she can
see
God or something through the dusty smoke
God or something burning, whistling
through the sky, like
embers of a fire
a fire
Click.

JACQLYN COPE

Jacqlyn Cope is an 8-year Air Force veteran that worked as an aeromedical evacuation mission controller who decided to leave the military in 2016 to pursue her writing career and education. She has an MFA in creative writing from Mount Saint Mary's University and is currently a 7th grade English teacher for LAUSD. Her work focuses on the catharsis of war stemming from her personal experience and others.

39. VULTURES
(inspired by The Raven)

I'm noticing vultures –
ugly hook-nosed hungry beaks,
razor claws eager to tear,
cold beady eyes set in tiny gruesome heads
tinged the color of blood,
bobbing atop chunky out-of-proportion bodies.

Silhouettes of wide wings circle,
rivaling the Reaper's flowing black cape,
seeking the decaying flesh of roadside kill:
the fallen, the aged, the mortally wounded,
the scent of death succulent as Sunday sauce.

They seem to follow me, gathering.

Ominous outlines flash in my periphery,
casting shadows on my consciousness.
Patiently focused, heartless eyes watch and wait.
They dot the sky like shorthand reminders of waning days,
bone-picking messiahs there to clean up after the party.

The sky darkens; my pace quickens –
I stumble, deafened by furious beating wings

my legs buckle

EVELYN HAMPTON

Evelyn Hampton (Wanamassa, NJ) is a member of the Jersey Shore Poets. Her publications include Monmouth Review, The Lyric, Poeming Pigeon and Stories of Music Vol I. She is inspired to take pen to paper by the restorative power of humor, music, nature and human connections.

40. ONLY THE MOON WAS WATCHING
(inspired by The Raven and A Dream within a Dream)

I said I'm leaving, and I don't know where I'm going
So I slammed the door shut and walked to an abandoned church
Whose sign read "SANCTUARY"
But there I found no peace
No sanctuary
No respite
I found nothing but the silence of a hot and humid night
It was there where only days before
I saw a dead baby bird who lay at the church's door
I thought and pondered and wondered and tried to make sense of it all,
I wanted to decipher the messages written on the hidden wall
I looked at the moon who's always watching, but still I could not make
sense of the messages the world was sending
More confused than ever before, I went back home and *gently* closed
the door

KRISTIN BROWN

I am a psychology graduate student who uses my interest in human nature, philosophy, as
well as my own tumultuous life experiences to inform my work.-Kristin

41. PESTICIDE
(inspired by The City in the Sea)

Feel me dig into your skin
Creeping and crawling within
Cutting the flow to your brain

An incision of the lungs
And you will depend on me
But I've only just begun

Carving out your bone marrow
Quenching my thirst with your blood
As it gushes from your veins

A collapse of the larynx
The words always suffocate T
hey're never able to breathe

I've drained all your muscle
No tissue left to wipe your eyes
Succumb to my infection

CHRIS WILSON

A creative writer in my spare time who loves to read dystopia novels and Edgar Allen Poe poetry and short stories.

42. YOUR GREATEST DANGER

o

The lights go out, you're all alone.
Your soul feels like it's lost its home.

Remaining calm is not a choice.
You've lost the power of your voice.

To scream would be the greatest option.
Next would be to breathe with caution.

For in the bed beside you, waiting,
lies your killer, meditating.

His body's calm. His eyes are patient.
Time's his friend. You can't out-wait him.

He plays a game of silent struggle.
Aren't guns part of all good cuddles?

But now you've sweated through the sheets,
sucking on your psyche's teet.

"No, please," you think, "just let me sleep!
I'll sow more love if peace I'll reap!"

And then, like that, a sudden end—
you wake and speak and breathe again.

But still you are your greatest danger—

BRIAN REYBURN

Brian Reyburn is an American writer of fiction, non-fiction, and poetry. He has a B.A. in Art History from University of Pittsburgh. He is the singer and primary song-writer of the indie-folk band Her Ladyship. His work has been featured by Grand Little Things and is forthcoming in SOFTBLOW Poetry Journal and Blood and Thunder Journal. Currently, he's working on his debut novel at his home in Pittsburgh, PA.

43. THE SENSATIONAL SHOW

Alone in the dressing room once more,
I peer through the keyhole at the onstage lore.
The ballerinas strike scythes at luminous mirrors.
The theatrical makeup turns to genuine horror.

I turn towards my gilded mirror- *oh!*
My bouquets wilt as a reverie *grows!*
A pallid beast emerges out of the glass.
She smells of old perfume and decayed sassafras.

I jiggle the brass doorknob until it frees me.
What do I witness? Several, shrieking banshees!
They chase the ballerinas, high on their toes.
The audience applauds, "It's all part of the show!"

I scamper down a spiral staircase
and throw open the theater doors. I embrace
an onyx forest that exhales a sanguine breath,
you've escaped a sensational death.

STEPHANIE LEE EVANS

Stephanie Lee Evans lives in Northeastern Pennsylvania. She studied Business and English at Pennsylvania State University, where she graduated in 2017. She enjoys writing both fiction and poetry.

44. CHARCUTERIE
(inspired by David Evans)

Hell stands waiting at the gate.
I dream I point, extend an arm, a finger pow! the bane evaporates
into dust,
I blow hot finger tips, smoky
as birthday candles
and walk away cool as Clint.

I awake kissed by a fist exploding my nose.

You saw me through a butcher's eye,
plucked from the clutch of new, green kids swelling the school
yard, fresh from the country kids.

Every morning whispered promises, finding, rendering; relishing
sly tearing of chicken wire across flesh;
artful bruising through jacket,
jumper, shirt, meat.

Token torture, stale breath: *More in store*. My fear engorged
you.

Alone in my bedroom your shank sharp outline persisted, spread,
diminished, scuttled.
My gagged heart screaming for help.
And no one came running.

Butcher boy, fear peddler: your face is gone now, indistinct as a
fist of grit. A nothing-face,
a name, a blank.

Menace is ripe.
I remember the taint of you.

DAVID W EVANS

D W Evans was born in Newcastle upon Tyne, and lives in Jersey. His poetry has been published by A3 Review and Bindweed, shortlisted and highly commended by Ó Bhéal and Acumen. He won the Alan Jones Memorial Prize 2019.

45. WHEN DEATH CAME

I begged.
Please, I said,
It's just me and my daughter. She's sick and
I'm all she has.
I need more time.

Take all the time you would like,

said Death.

I am not here for you.

TIM GENOVESI

Tim Genovesi is an OK web developer, a helicopter dog dad, a poor gardener, and a recent shut in, though not always in that order. He holds a Bachelor of Arts in English / Creative Writing from Weber State University in Ogden, Utah.

46. MR. QUIET

As I drove down 303, I nearly breathed myself into a coma, hyperventilating
through the dim midnight lights.

I had just watched *Midsommar*, and my stomach stretched itself back to a previous winter,
when it was empty, and I swallowed every second of the day like a full meal.

And I could feel him, I watched him,
amorphous head set atop my shoulder, as if
embracing me from behind, as if he *was* the car seat,
but when I looked down at his arms,

they stretched out in front of me. And his blackened fingers twisted
in every which
direction before all looping back
into my chest.
I could feel them peeking between
every muscle,

looking for something in the viscera. And when he'd pull, I lurched forward, wanting to vomit,
vomit out the infidelity. But nothing came.

And as he laughed his faceless laugh, I breathed in the concrete
facts, and out the paranoia.
With each breath, his laugh faded

and the streetlights returned.

EARL MINOZA

Earl Minoza is a New York based writer and a recent graduate of St.Thomas Aquinas
College, during which he was a contributor editor to Odyssey Online and editor-in-chief of
Voyager while also majoring in both psychology and creative writing. His works explore
the relationship and intersectionality of sex, power, violence, religion, and how the
intersections of these ideas and the emotions that accompany them define the human
experience.

47. THEY ALL LIE

Steal
Cheat
Beg
Pray
Talk
Shit.

And there I sat looking up at what I thought was *hope*
Oh boy I couldn't have been Anymore wrong
They said it would work, but it never did
They said it be okay, but they were wrong
They gave me so much faith,
Just give it time, but I hate them all
Then I took a chance
And the teacher said wow
That is deep
I should have never cared, but **I couldn't help it**
And I wish my **I died there**
I hoped they were serious
I really thought **I learned**
I was so dam happy I ran around like a crazy
Saying look I did it I finally know how write
I was so naïve.
I started making poems and even try a novel. I took them to a person
that once help me in the past
She told me oh you have to get these out there
she was so encouraging
So, I shared them online
They told me these are really amazing !!!

But In the end, **I realized,**
I should have just Buried them all.

BRYAN HENNIG

Writing and grammar is my number 1 enemy. though i have a lot of poems and short stories that normally fall apart because of typos and wrong pretence. it helps me vent my ever long daydreaming self.

48. BIRDMAN
(inspired by Alone)

I would often
lay
There
On
My bed

a mad kid,
burning bridges
to sanity

match
after
match

like
the loneliest prisoner
this world
has never
seen.

And the
White
Flickers
As I watch the ceiling

Dreams
In
Black
And white

Ideas
Start living

Sad, little creatures,
stories

And
I
Wait
A little longer
To give them all
A
name.

ULRICH RABE

My name is Ulrich Rabe. I am a writer of short fiction and poetry, born and raised in Germany. The voices in literature that enthralled me were Kafka, Céline, Fante, Bukowski - probably the cornerstones of my own writing.-Ulrich

49. A BIRD IN THE HAND
(inspired by The Raven)

It is me who flies first,
but in the end I'll forget.

Scrape and shift.
Squelch and score.
Shattered skin, red
shrieks and tears.
I soar up. I fall down.
And you are conceived.

You start as bone
sore, swollen and whole.

I misplace my heart
in my palm as you
crown my wrist with
an egg-shaped dome.
Animated and shell
shocked, I watch as

You crack from within
and I crack from without.

Slice and scratch.
Split and sear.
Speckled egg, blue
plumes and razors
I am raw. I am food.
And you are hungry.

It is you who flies last
and that's all I remember.

SARAH STRETTON

Sarah Stretton writes flash fiction, short stories and poetry. She has been published in Oxford Poetry journal, Popshot Quarterly and MIRonline and is the winner of the Saveas International Prose Prize 2019. She has placed as runner up in the Retreat West Microfiction competition and is currently longlisted for the Primadonna Prize 2020.

50. FRIGHT CEMETERY

I may have gone outside,
but I do not know,
if today

the reckoning
worth my redemption

living old and ugly
is humid Cairo
only green, blue, red

the streets are not de Janeiro
they liven with a ceremonial understatement

But each cemetery,
Hemisphere North—Hemisphere South,
one and the same

even as our honey world spinneth people turn, turn in graves
for it is now a cursed earth, its mists are acid rain

JUSTIN-PAUL STARLIN

Justin-Paul Starlin writes poetry and is from Northern California; he has been a passionate
writer for just over ten years and his work has been published in Strange Horizons, The
Write Launch, and Wingless Dreamer. He hopes to release a first chapbook sometime later
this year.

51. BLACK
(inspired by The Raven)

One word many meanings
each one a part of this life.

Night
black

Him
black

Mama!
I gave them the truth
like you told me to mama

Mama!
You said I would be okay if I
followed the rules mama

My skin lied, mama.
The words from my mouth fell apart
when my skin
broke the silence.

The cold needle
piercing his skin. silent. night. **black**
Black.
I see you mama.

SHVETHAA JAYAKUMAR

Shvethaa Jayakumar is a junior majoring in Political Science and Labor Studies at Rutgers University, studying to become a lawyer. She has been writing for the past 8 years, and really enjoys the beauty in how stories are crafted. Her article, "Apparently, Licking An Ice Cream Tub Is Worse Than Raping An Unconscious Girl" was featured on the Odyssey Trending Page at the #1 spot, and was read over 19,000 times. In her spare time, she loves to watch films and spend time with her dog, Disco.

52. DIRGE
(inspired by The Raven)

If I could just walk out that door, I told myself
I will never ever take a step back.
I want no more violence that shook me to the core,
that feasted on all the tears swelling in my soul,
for my eighteen years of life.

8 years of deliberation over desperation.
I walked out that door of our 7th floor apartment
with 6 books constricted in a shit-colored worn
suitcase that matched my mood perfectly.
5 am, I took the first bus across the snow-covered town
where 4 is the number symbolized death
that no one liked. Like me.
I picked up my 3 luggage and there I was,
pretending I knew what I was signing up for.
I took away with me 2 dreams on my 1st flight
And, with a fake smile of confidence
that depicted, *I'll be alright, bye, mom and dad*
I mustered the courage to say not a word

I was transported to Long Beach, LA. United States.
What a change of sight from a world I saw only gray
to a place where the sun didn't know what else to do
but shine. I snuggled up the warmth from the giant yellow star
every day, until I was shaken by the amount of
blissful uncertainty that accumulated - the youth
yearning and the consequential feeling of
eternal indecision.
But the sun melted any anxiety before I could
dwell and contemplate the future
it felt so good I had to squeeze my cheek
to make sure it wasn't all just a dream
p.s. it wasn't.

YIYA WANG

A first-generation English speaker, immigrant who migrated to the US on my own at 18. Now a fulltime first-gen college student at a California community college. Have big dreams and a daring heart. Also a blogger, Couchsurfer, founder of my college's first Poetry Club, Quoran with 1.8K followers, and the mother of an awesome 2-year-old.

53. SHE WORE HER MOURNING NOON AND NIGHT
(inspired by Alone)

She wore her mourning noon and night
through dark of thunder, lightning bright... .

She eagerly awaits the next downpour to go keening
as others await movies or Christmas...To sit in plain sight
– yet obscure in her widow's weeds – and wantonly unleash another
cleansing torrent of sobbing saline catharsis.

Thus, this day, she sits alone in that quiet, dust-to-dust place,
on that unyielding cement bench, wailing into the booming, cracking
thunder – unheard – emptying those limpid green vessels anew unseen–
until... "I am renewed!" she cries.

Renewed. Energized. Not drained and weakened.
(Glimpsing the scars on her indelibly craggy left arm reminds her
of that prior, "less subtle," approach which had wickedly betrayed her.)

As always, after today's ritual, before returning to her drab
domicile of Karmic Loneliness, she nips over the myriad of gnarled
roots onto the smooth puddled walkway to scan, through swollen eyes,
the benevolent dark clouds.

The Bearded Countenance that returns her gaze is smiling, too.
As always.

TONIA KALOURIA

Tonia loves humor and rhyme, but also Darkness and Poe. Her poem based on The Raven is
in the Anthology Quoth the Raven. Her dark though humorous poem Heavy Metal Band;
Iron Clad Contract is featured July 15 on Fox Hollow Stories.

54. THE RISING STEAM
(inspired by The Raven)

Twisted along

A black burning

Road,

Coursed to a

Fanning wind

Quieting the

Rising steam…

KATHERINE ROBBINS KARR

Katherine Robbins Karr grew up in a small town in Northern NJ where people did not dream of becoming artists. She is a singer/musician in a duo called Love Lyzardz, and a published poet with a degree in Creative Writing from Mills College. She lives in SF with her partner Haji and dog Aly.

55. ANOTHER WORD FOR MISERY
(inspired by *A Dream within a Dream, Epigram for Wall Street, In Youth I have known for*)

I shot the canary on my window pane
The kickback with 22 tufts of rind and feathers
Mostly tannic and dusted plumes, the thick black blood
Flumed shallow, cascaded through the louvred furnace vent below

Opened - with no wherewithal
Yet how these thoughts still, keep me up at night

I once heard there was another word for misery
Like a second set of keys hushed in your grandfather's cigar case But I must be mistaking since the bells all toll
When the cannons summoned the bodies of water one last time

But then again, have you ever felt the fresh loam rumble Or seen a tombstone split?
Pretending to befriend ol' Lazarus is a stake in the temple An olive branch swallowed with all its pits

Death has all the Seven Seals
Working with God against the grain
She's the grey from the clouds on the lowest shelf As the veil grows long and thin
The asphyxiation of silence
She goes by any other name

CASEY SIMPSON

Casey Simpson is a cellar assistant at a cidery. She is an avid hiker, trail runner, and mountain biker with a fierce conservationist heart. On most evenings after work, she can be found walking and philosophizing on the nature paths towards the outskirts of town with her bow tie wearing pup, Wolfie. She lives in Northampton, Massachusetts.

56. DEPRESSION
(inspired by Alone)

detention
pressed into the mind
captured in a caption
more than an indentation
a pit
a deterrence from opening more
no prison bars or bottles of alcohol
are worse than the chosen room
an empty cavity in a living house
with a lock you lock
a door you press your ear against
a bed you sleep in most of the time
a wait to miss another day
at night you live while everyone sleeps
day is wrong
it plagues with what-ifs and why-nots
for the sunrise gives no comfort
no matter how it tries to fill you
the endless solitary
dominates the cortex.

ROBERT FARMER

Robert Farmer is an aspiring worker of words. He currently hails from North Middletown, NJ. He enjoys writing, no matter how painful it can be. If only to keeps us thinking, questioning our doubts of ourselves. His poetry does this for him. He hopes it will do the same for you.

57. BIG GAME
(inspired by A Dream within a Dream)

an ale-faded great
lodges cartridge
lowers muzzle
sun glaring
gags himself
seeing death
as something other
than stuff.

an ambling giant
claws retracted
crushes fronds
on safari.
the startled beast
begins his death-rush;
a man keeps both
eyes open &
blasts. Parting round,
his rugged crown
strewn art

MOLLY FELTH

Molly Felth is a Connecticut, USA poet. Her writing appears in *H_NGM_N Journal and Eve Poetry Magazine*.

58. CHARLIE NORTON'S GRAVE

The old lady stumbled up the cemetery hill, over piles of twigs and
broken bark
with Charlie Norton's grave ahead, and Charlie Norton still in it.
Death is like a thumbtack, she thought. *The harder you push, the more
you secure the picture.*

The girl she knew in high school was there, handcuffed to a tree and
pleading
while vultures and buzzards circled above her, screaming in the
twilight's dimming.
Death is like a marathon, she thought. *The faster the rac,e the quicker
you get to the finish.*

The boys she knew in high school were there, drinking with the girls by
the getaway car
then relieving themselves on old Charlie's grave, in a dare for the ghost to
waken.
Death is like a latrine, the lady thought. *The longer you wait, the
messier it gets.*

A flat frog lay on the marble gravestone, stiff and crisp as bacon.
She kicked it flipside, drank another ale, and then squatted to do her
business.
Death is a fright, and I deserve this, she thought. *I deserve this for the
things I've done.*

For the boys, the beers and the getaway car, and for daring the ghost to
waken
For the pleading and the tree, the handcuffs and the girl
and the vultures in the twilight's dimming

I deserve this she thought, as she stumbled down the hill
over piles of twigs and broken bark
with Charlie Norton's grave behind her, and
Charlie Norton not in it.

C. CROPANI

C. Cropani grew up near Boston, MA, but became bi-coastal after attending the University of California, Santa Cruz. She began writing on buses, trains and planes during her travels back and forth across the country. You can find her making brooms, binding books and holding experimental poetry jams at her shop in Salem, MA. She is also working on her first chapbook. Contact C. Cropani at WordWitchLiterary.com

59. MY OWN ANNABEL LEE
(inspired by Annabel Lee)

If love was the shelter, she was the storm
Her quiet embrace, deep, long and warm
If time, an illusion and this world a dream Then silence dear lover, and
let me be asleep Her hair long and thin
Her face pale and drawn
Her eyes as innocent, as the newborn fawn
The lips that tasted of roses, blood red and sweet
Were so dainty and drawn, they dare not be used to eat
Meant as they were, for soft utterances and long sighs
For endless daydreams and put off goodbyes
It was in this way I saw her, as she fell back to sleep
Into the darkness so black and the abyss so deep
One final drop of the poison, did slide from those lips
As I whispered goodbye, my lips to her fingertips
For the love that she had, could 'ere be anyones but mine
And for this crime alone, she was sentenced to die
I could not allow, her sweet touch or embrace
To grace the temple of another, as they felt her caress on their face
For mine evermore, she will always be
Perfect in her estrangement, my own Annabel Lee.

BETHANY BARTON

Bethany is an LA based author and freelance writer. She recently completed her first book,
Apologies I Never Got, a book about learning to write our own apologies, for the ones we
never got. The book is due for release soon. She enjoys writing about the human experience
expressed through the emotions that connect us; loss, love, sorrow, joy, suffering,
confusion, elation etc. She especially enjoys writing in the realms of philosophy, and
relationships and has recently had several pieces of poetry and flash fiction published.

60. SHADOW MAN
(inspired by Alone)

He waits in the darkest corner in the corner of your eye,
you only sense his presence and you barely question why,
he wears a cloak of shadows while a-playing with your mind,
but when you turn to see him there is nothing left to find.

When you feel his icy gaze it trickles down your spine,
it wavers on your empty neck and brushes like a vine,
it fiddles with your senses while he's whispering your name -
you know not why he comes to you, nor how to play his game.

His eyes glint in the darkness as he calls you from your sleep,
his fingers stroke the window but you hardly hear him creep,
he slips beneath a creaking bed or finds a hiding place,
yet when you know his company he'll leave without a trace.

Forever just beyond your grasp and just beyond your sight,
he's always just behind you - lurking day and night.
Forever in the corner and yet never there at all -
you feel his omnipresence like the writing on a wall.

MONICA YELL

Monica is a theatre student from Sussex, England, who is always up for a chilling foray into Edgar Allan Poe's writing, provided that the chill doesn't extend to her accompanying cup of tea. Previously commended by Young Poets Network for her emulation of Edward Lear's nonsense poetry, she hopes to one day channel her love for being inspired by other poets into becoming one herself.

61. FREE FALL

I could say I'm dying of loneliness
like my brave single friends
some of my partnered ones too
        I know the hell of years of tractionless stall
or that I lost my job (with no savings)
so after paying the rent
there's almost nothing left for food
like those old people in grocery stores
who hold up a can, hesitate,
slowly put it back on the shelf
        I've shopped like that
memories of worse times
filed in my album of complaints
fuel the fantasy
that the past is over
but it's barely begun

DION FARQUHAR

Dion Farquhar is a poet who has recent poems in Blind Field, Mortar, Birds Piled Loosely, Local Nomad, Columbia Poetry Review, Shampoo, moria, Shifter, BlazeVOX, etc. Her second poetry book Wonderful Terrible was published by Main Street Rag Publishing in 2013, her second chapbook Snap came out in 2017 at Crisis Chronicles Press, and her third chapbook Just Kidding was published by Finishing Line Press in 2018. She works as an exploited adjunct at two universities, but still loves the classroom, and she is active in the University of California Santa Cruz adjunct union, the UC-AFT.

62. THE PANTYHOSE MAN

Visions from my past continue
to haunt me.
Late in night when the rest of you sleep,
I lie in my bed afraid he'll appear.
It's been years since it happened,
though it feels like only yesterday.
Yet again,
I find myself paralyzed in my bed.
The man reappears cloaked in all black,
staring me down from the foot of my bed.
Pantyhose stretched tight
worn over his head.
I'm too frightened to move,
is he real or just a nightmare?
It's been years since the pantyhose man
began haunting my sleep.
And late at night while the rest of you dream,
I'm haunted again
by the pantyhose man.

JENNIFER AYALA

Jennifer Ayala is a Texan native, born in Big Spring, Texas. In her adolescent age she moved to Houston, Texas with her family, although her roots are still deeply embedded in the West Texas soil. Jennifer's love for writing came to her when she was just a young girl and has since blossomed into her most trusted outlet of self-discovery and truth where she allows the pen to bleed from her heart the most vulnerable thoughts within her. Becoming a mother has been one of her greatest life's joys, and it is with utmost importance that she teaches her children resilience, hard work, perseverance and the ambition to always believe in themselves. Through her work as a writer and poet, Jennifer hopes that she can comfort others through the art of writing simply by the relief it provides being able to express oneself through the usage of words.

63. LENORE, THE BACKSTORY

She had been for thirty years
the wife of my best friend

Dark nights were darker still,
no day so bright to cheer
my shadowed rooms

a lovers' heart
is most in pain
when holding close
what it must keep concealed

She and I had only once
—that and nevermore—
a thought of our romance revealed

To fortify, she took three sips
of his Amontillado

then took her life to gain that place
where I might be, were I not still
too cowardly to follow

ALAN MEYROWITZ

Alan Meyrowitz retired in 2005 after a career in computer research. His writing has appeared
in *Dark Ink Anthology, Eclectica, Esthetic Apostle, Existere, From Whispers to Roars,
Inwood Indiana, Jitter, The Literary Hatchet, The Nassau Review, Poetry Quarterly,
Schuylkill Valley Journal, Shark Reef, Shroud, Spirit's Tincture*, and others.

64. BONES II

When the pathologist put my naked body on a slab
And tried to analyse what it was I had
He put his hand under my chin
Then caressed me right down to my shin
He touched me with a loving precision so profound
But so mundane and accustomed to his job underground
But you see my skin was soft and looked quite fresh
However what dwelt within proved I had deceiving flesh
As he made his incisions and opened me wide
He found that there were old bones inside
He noted my bones that were cracked and split
Then regarded my face once more that was not so telling of this He
sewed up my dead skin, zipped me up and put me back
Put me in the draw, closed it and left it at that
But the thing he could not have known that my dead body did hide Was
that when he touched my skin,
That was the love I never felt whilst I were alive

MOREMI

Moremi a British Poet, Novelist, and short story Writer, specialising in free verse poetry, coming of age, drama, chick-lit and fantasy stories, and novels. Bones II deals with the heartache of the life in which we all dwell now, mixed with the wonder of how we will be remembered and the legacy our lives will leave behind, the two stitched together with a dark, macabre twist. Moremi has been writing poetry and stories since childhood, always with a love for the mundane mixed with a dash of fantasy. All of Moremi's works are a commentary on life and the many paths one may take on the turn of a dime. What the future holds for this young writer?. . .The world.

65. DEN, BLACK, K, CAT

we cats love possessing   stretching objects with our minds
and I'll play with my   shell,
the wife's neck;
/
human teeth don't regenerate, yet Berenice is a future cyborg,
same loop as those in my book's spine;
/
me, avian humanoid, performing mind possession on Nestlé's trading mark,
under mask, colour red
— stop — you, ancestors of Henri Nestlé, are welcomed to visit anytime,
to see how we master death itself in 28th century;
/
you see, my blue friend was an eyeball
with light blue iris who had just accepted another surgery case with me,
and I, was the tell-tale heart;
/
as a distorted raven mask, I've been alive,
Montresor didn't kill Fortunato,
didn't notice my liveliness and the material of extreme flexibility I cast,
turning F into a fork, one alive;
/
from now on, only the greyer-grey is privileged enough
to be   gyrating through   avoidances
on expiration date of your fleshes,   essence of dark,   deprivation,
nothing thaws in nothingness outside.

FRANZ LOECRHENN

Franz Loecrhenn is a cyborg-bard constantly second-drafting his symptoms, the first draft of his dystopian novel included. He was once based in Glasgow, Scotland, where he was heavily influenced by the amazing art culture, accent and beyond. Intrigued by the mechanism behind this world, his brain has been in synch with theories from the likes of Roland Barthes, Jacques Derrida as well as Lao Tze. He believes that the ideas of nothingness and deconstruction are applicable to the reality and could distribute to reconstructing a fascinating world, the embodiment of the aforementioned first draft he's been in close contact with where ancient language is introduced and spatial-time cracks are created. He is now an academic English teacher at UNSW Global Education, scaffolding his way to one day become a published novelist who could, through this works, help share and alleviate the growing pains from loneliness and depression amongst contemporary societies.

66. KISS ME NOW

Kiss me now, before I die
So I may welcome Death
With the taste of living on my breath.

And Death, in turn, will wonder why
The threat of his assured embrace
Cannot erase the trace of your desire on my face.

You, upon my lips, cheeks, eyes, ears, skin;
Then swear, with Death, that it's a sin
For any god to summon him to take me in.

Take me quick!
His darkest room awaits,
For I assume he will consume
    even a girl in bloom.

MARINA FAVILA

Marina Favila is an English professor emerita at James Madison University in Virginia. She has published essays on Shakespeare, poetry, and film in various academic journals. Her published creative work includes pieces in *Weirdbook, The Mythic Circle, Wraparound South,* Harvardwood's *Seven Deadly Sins* anthology and Flame Tree Press's *Haunted House Short Stories.*

" *Believe in yourself* "

"I want to use this opportunity to thank all the participants, Winglessdreamer's team and community members to make this publication possible. Thanks for the support and well-wishes."
–Ruchi Acharya (Wingless Dreamer Founder)

WRITE. FEEL. PUBLISH

If you liked our work, kindly do give us reviews on Amazon.com/winglessdreamer. It will mean a lot to our editorial team. You can also tag or follow us on:

Instagram: @winglessdreamer1 @ruchi_acharya

Facebook: www.facebook.com/winglessdreamer

Mail us: Editor: editor@winglessdreamer.com

Sales: sales@winglessdreamer.com

Website: www.winglessdreamer.com

You can also support our small creative community through donation: www.paypal.me/winglessdreamer

BOOKS PUBLISHED BY WINGLESS DREAMER

Passionate Penholders

Passionate Penholders II

Art from heart

Daffodils

Father and I

Sunkissed

Tunnel of lost stories

Overcoming Fear

The Rewritten

Fruits of our Quarantine   Magic of motivational   Diversity

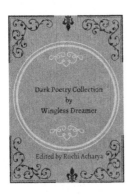

Dark poetry collection